STOP!

DON'T BUY THIS BOOK!
At least, not yet.

The basic rules for the Micro Chapbook RPG system and Hammer + Cross found in this book can be downloaded for FREE through DriveThruRPG.com in the Manor of Blood book. Give the system a try before you buy.

With that in mind, this Deluxe Adventure Module includes everything you need to play the game.

You don't need any other book to experience the game!

Voyage of the Vampire

DELUXE ADVENTURE MODULE

The Lord Vandrac Chronicles V.4

An Adventure Module for 1 Player
For the Hammer + Cross RPG
Designed by Noah Patterson

Hammer Cross

Voyage of the Vampire
The Lord VanDrac Chronicles V.4
Copyright © 2020 Noah Patterson
ISBN: 9798698817314

Contents

Section 1.0

What is Voyage of the Vampire?

Voyage of the Vampire is an adventure module for the Hammer + Cross Roleplaying game system and is the fourth volume in the Lord

VanDrac Chronicles story arc. Each volume in the 5 book series stands on its own, but all connect to create a greater campaign. Therefore, this adventure can be played on its own or as part of the larger VanDrac story arc.

This book includes the basic rules to allow you to play the game. However, the Hammer + Cross core rulebook will go into greater detail on all elements of the game. Hammer + Cross uses the Micro Chapbook RPG system and, therefore, this book can be combined with any other books or genres in the same system.

For those new to the system, Micro Chapbook RPG is an ultra-rules light fantasy-based game designed specifically for the solitaire gamer in mind--but is adaptable for co-op play as well as traditional Game Master driven gameplay. Hammer + Cross is a Gothic Horror rendition of the traditionally fantasy-based game system. In Hammer + Cross, you take on the role of vampire and monster hunters in an alternate version of late 1800s Victorian Europe where evil abounds. The game is strongly influenced by the Hammer Horror films of the 60s and 70s.

Section 2.0

What Do You Need?

To play this adventure you will need:

- A Pencil and Eraser
- A Sheet of Graph Paper
- A Character Sheet
- 2 Six-Sided Dice
- This Adventure Book
- The Hammer + Cross Core Rulebook (Optional).

Section 3.0

Rules Basics

Hammer + Cross is an ultra-simple roleplaying game that can be played solo (or with a traditional GM if you so wish). In the next few pages, you will find the basic rules for the game system:

What You Need: 2 six-sided dice, graph paper, notepaper/character sheet, a pencil w/eraser, Scenario Maps/Sticker, this chapbook.

Rolling: During play, you always roll 1D6, trying to score equal to or lower than your stat score. If you are proficient, roll 2 dice and take the better result of the 2. 1 always succeeds. 6 always fails. (NOTE: When you see 1D3 it means you roll a die and half the result rounding up. 1D2 means: Odds = 1, Evens = 2.)

Characters: To create a character, do the following:
1. **STATS:** You have 4 statistics. **ST**rength, **DE**xterity, **WI**ts, **CH**arisma. You have 7 points to assign between them as you see fit (9 for an easier game). No stat can have a score lower than 1 or higher than 4 at this point.
2. **CLASS:** Choose a class. There are 4 to choose from. Each one will make you proficient in one area.
   a. **Soldier:** Proficient in ST
   b. **Hunter:** Proficient in DE
   c. **Nurse/Doctor:** Proficient in WI
   d. **Priest/Nun:** Proficient in CH

3. **ORDER:** Choose an Order to join. Your Order grants you a +1 bonus to one stat.
   a. **Order of the Hammer:** +1 ST
   b. **Order of the Dagger:** +1 DE
   c. **Order of the Cross:** +1 WI
   d. **Order of the Sun:** +1 CH
4. **HEALTH, WILL, & FAITH:** Your health is your ST+DE+20. Your will is your WI+CH+20. Your Faith is your Wits + 20 (+ 25 if you're a Priest/Nun).

Weapons: Roll 2D6 to determine your money. You may buy equipment now. Weapons have a damage rating and a cost in pounds (£). Below are some basic starter weapons, both ranged and melee. You may have 2 melee and 1 ranged at any given time. You may buy these and others in town as well.

Melee Weapons			Ranged Weapons		
Dagger	1	1g	Holy Cross	1	2g
Wooden Stake	1D3	2g	Holy Water Sprayer	1D3	3g
Hammer	1D3+1	3g	Rusty Revolver	1D3+1	5g
Cane Sword	1D6	4g	Blessed Long Whip	1D6	6g
Silver Sword	1D6+1	5g	Crossbow	1D6+1	7g

Armor and Items: Armor grants the wearer a boost to their health, will, or both. Other items such and food and potions can be used to restore lost health and will. On the next page are some basic starter items and armors. You may buy these and others in town as well.

Armor			Items		
Shield	+3H	1£	(2) Bread Crust	1D3 H	1£
Top Hat	+3W	1£	(3) Wine	1D3 W	1£
Black Cloak	+6H	2£	(4) Steak Meal	1D6 H	2£
Chainmail	+6W	2£	(5) Holy Water	1D6 W	2£
Blessed Robes	+6HW	3£	(6) Miracle	FULL HW	6£

Generating Rooms: Begin by choosing a random square on the graph paper and generating the first room. To generate a room, roll 2D6. The number rolled in the number of squares in the room. These can be drawn in any way, shape, or form so long as they are orthogonally connected. Next, roll 1D3 (1D6 divided by 2 rounded up). This is the number of NEW doors in the room (not including the door you just came through). Draw small rectangles to represent the doors along any single square's edge to designate an exit.

Room Type: Each newly generated room has a type. Roll 1D6 on the scenario Room Chart to determine the type. Note this in the room with the type's letter code as listed on the chart.

Doorways: Next, you will choose one door to move through into the next room. Roll 1D6 to determine the door type. After moving, generate the new room. (This chart is also provided in each scenario).

(5–6)	Unlocked	Move through freely.
(4)	Stuck	Must make a ST check to get through. Lose 1 WILL to reroll and try again.
(3)	Locked	Must make a WI check to get through. Lose 1 WILL to reroll and try again.
(1–2)	Trapped	Must make a WI check to disarm and move. If you fail, take 1D3 damage but still move through.

Monsters: After Entering any room. Roll to generate the monsters in the room. Roll once for the monster type (on the scenario Monster Chart) and a second time for the number of that monster. Each monster has a Max number of that type that can appear in a room, a Health Damage, a Will Damage, and a Life Force. **Vampires** also have two additional special stats:

- **Bloodletting (BL):** Each time the player rolls a 6 during a melee attack (an instant failure), the vampire bites them and drinks their blood. The BL is how much LF it regains.
- **Power (P):** This is the mental strength of the vampire. It is the amount of faith the player will lose if they fail during the Faith check.

Fighting: To fight the monsters in your room, follow these steps in order:

1. **Bravery:** Make a CH check. If you pass, gain 1 Will. If you fail, you lose Will according to the monster's W DMG. If your Will is ever 0, all rolls take a +1 modifier. (A roll of 1 STILL always succeeds)
2. **Ranged Attack:** IF the room is 4 squares or larger you may make a ranged attack. Roll a DE check. If you succeed, apply weapon damage to the monster's LF.

3. **Melee Attack:** You MUST now make a melee attack using a ST check. If you succeed, apply the weapon's damage to the monster's LF. If you fail, roll the H DMG for one monster and apply it to your health. If you have a second melee weapon equipped, attack again.
4. **Repeat:** Repeat this entire process until either you die or you've killed all the monsters in the room. Run away with a successful CH roll.

Faith Check: After battle, if the player was bitten by a vampire during combat, that player makes a WI check. If the player fails, they lose Faith in the amount of the vampire's power. The player may spend 1 Willpower to reroll this check. If Faith reaches 0, the character dies and becomes a vampire.

Search: After battle roll 1D6. If you get 1 through 5 you earn that much money. If you roll a six, roll on the Items table included in the scenario (or the one here in this section. The number to the left of each item is the search roll number). If you roll a 1 on the items chart you find nothing.

The Boss: The boss of the dungeon will not appear until you've encountered all the other monsters in the scenario at least once. Additionally, it will only appear in specific room types as outlined in each scenario. If you roll the boss when it can't appear, reroll. Once the boss is defeated, the game ends.

Alternate Boss Rule: (for potentially quicker games) Keep track of each monster you kill during the dungeon. After each battle is won, roll 2D6. If the roll is LOWER than the number of monsters killed during the dungeon, the boss can now have a chance of appearing. The boss will only appear in specific areas, as designated by the scenario rules. If you roll the boss when it can't appear, reroll.

Leveling Up: In between games you may spend 100 gold to add +1 to one stat (or 50 for an easier game). No stat can be higher than 5. For an easier game, simply level up whenever you defeat a boss. You may also buy new equipment. You may only have 2 melee and 1 ranged weapon at a time.

Section 4.0

Adventure Background

Having gained knowledge that the bones of an ancient vampire, Lord VanDrac, is heading by ship to the new world, you don't wait to get approval from your supervisor at The Order to further pursue this case. With the knowledge that a cult of possible followers is working to resurrect the once great vampire lord, you don't feel you have time to ponder on the next course of action. You must track down the ship and board it before it can disembark for the Americas. You just pray you can get there in time.

Section 5.0

The Docks

Your carriage rattles at top speed through the cobblestone streets of London, rocking you violently back and forth. You had wondered for some time why The Order insisted on using this rude and less than reliable carriage service, but now it is becoming clear. They are willing to drive recklessly and at top speeds to achieve the goals of The Order. It is times like this when such recklessness and speed is necessary. You make a mental note to tip the driver heavily next time you see him.

The London Docks come into view, a steaming, teaming, confusion of large ships and small boats alike loading and unloading cargo and passengers alike. A light drizzle drives a few people indoors to the warehouses and shipping buildings. However, most continue to work.

"Stop here," You shout. The carriage comes to a startling halt, nearly throwing you out of your seat. Using the momentum, you throw open the door and leap out. A sense of dread overwhelms you as you look at the sheer amount of ships in dock. How will you find the correct one in time?

Dock Special Rules:

Limited Map: Before starting to play, draw in the "starting rooms" (including Dock 1 and Warehouse 1) as shown below.

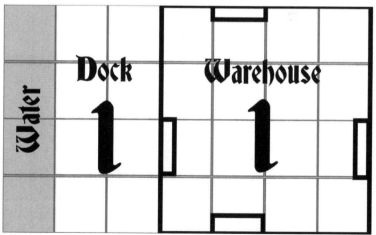

This should be drawn at the very bottom of your graph paper. During gameplay, you begin on Dock 1. From there you can move into Warehouse 1 or North onto Dock 2. Whenever you move North you will build a duplicate of the Dock/Warehouse pictured on the previous page, only adding in the next numerical number. The docks can't reach above 10.

Alleyways: If you move out of any Warehouse through the east door you will be taken into the alleyways. When in the alleyways, roll as normal for rooms and doors. However, the alleyways cannot exceed 5 squares in width. Rooms rolled must be built in the confines of that space.

Doors: You will never make a door roll when moving from one dock to another. However, when you move through a door attached to a warehouse at all you will roll on the Warehouse Doors chart. When you move from one alleyway to another you will roll on the Alleyway Exits chart.

Dock Room Types: Docks have no room type. They are simply the docks. If you get into a fight on the docks, during melee combat, after a successful attack, you may roll a second ST check to try and push the enemy in the water, thus removing them from battle. However, if you fail the melee roll, make a DE check. If you fail, you get pushed off into the water yourself. On the next round of combat, during the ranged step, make a DE check to swim and climb out of the water. If you fail, the enemy attacks from the docks, dealing damage. Skip the melee step while you are in the water.

Warehouse and Alleyway Room Types: The warehouse and alleyways have their own room type tables, although shorter. They both require a D3 roll instead of the regular D6.

Rolling Monsters: The monster chart is the same for all 3 sections of the map. However, When on the docks, subtract −2 from the roll. When in the Warehouse, roll normally. When in the alleyways, roll +2.

Locating the Ship: Before beginning play, take 10 Room Number Trackers (sheet included at the end of the book). Randomize them face down and draw 1 without looking. Set that aside. That is the numbered Dock where the ship is. Keep the others facedown and nearby. The Monster chart has the possibility of rolling up a "Dock Worker." When this happens, you will have no combat encounter or search roll. Instead, you will try to find out information about the ship by making a CH roll. If you pass, draw 1 room marker and look at it. You now know that number isn't the dock you are looking for. If you fail, the dock worker leaves. If you roll a natural 6, the dock worker attacks you as you made him mad.

<u>The Ship is Leaving:</u> After completing a room, make a note of 1 "Ship Disembark" point. Then roll 2D6. Treat one die as the 10s, and the other as the 1s. (So a roll of 6 and 1 would be 61.) If the roll is less than the number of "Ship Disembark" points, the ship leaves and you fail the investigation. You can start the scenario over and try again.

Warehouse Doorways

5-6	**Unlocked**	Move through freely.
3-4	**Stuck**	Must make a ST check to get through. Lose 1 WILL to reroll and try again.
1-2	**Locked**	Must make a WI check to get through. Lose 1 WILL to reroll and try again.

Alleyway Exit

6	**Archway**	Move through freely.
5	**Strong Iron Gate**	A heavy iron gate blocks the way. Must make a WI check to pick the lock. If you fail, lose 1 WILL and reroll and try again.
3-4	**Rusted Iron Gate**	A rusted iron gate blocks the way. Must make a ST check to break the lock. If you fail, lose 1 WILL and reroll and try again.
1-2	**Blocked**	A stack of boxes, barrels, trash, or crates block the way. Make a DE check to climb over. If you fail, lose 1 HEALTH and reroll to try again.

Warehouse Room Types

1	Sparse	S	There are very few cargo items in here. It makes it easy to maneuver. No special effects.
2	Cluttered	C	This warehouse is cluttered with cargo and items seemingly tossed haphazardly here and there. This makes combat difficult. +1 on all attacks.
3	Full	F	This warehouse is filled to the brim with cargo from ships, but it all seems very well organized. During combat, everyone can take cover. +1 on ranged combat attacks, but −1 (to a minimum of 1) H−DMG from enemies.

Alleyway Area Types

1	Empty	E	This alleyway is clear of debris and empty. No effect.
2	Trash	T	Piles of trash and barrels have been dumped here. The smell of old fish and rot permeates. Each time you fail a bravery roll, lose +1 Will.
3	Foggy	F	This alley is filled with smoke and fog, making it hard to see. No ranged attacks are allowed. Melee attacks are made at a +1 modifier.

Dock Monsters					
#	Monster	Max	H-DMG	W-DMG	LF
1	No Monster	–	–	–	–
2	Dock Worker*	1	1D3	1	5
3	Bat	4	1D2	1D3+1	3
4	Dock Worker*	1	1D3	1	5
5	Plague Rat+	4	1D2	1D2	3
6	Thug	3	1D3+1	1D2	7
7	Dock Worker*	1	1D3	1	5
8	Red Cultist-	1	1D6	1D6	15

*Dock Workers only attack if you roll a natural 6 during the CH check.

+Plague Rats have a chance of giving you the plague. When you take H-DMG from one, make a ST check to resist the disease. If you fail, you have the plague. All incoming H-DMG does +1. Upon entering a new room, make a WI check to administer medicine to yourself. If you pass, you rid yourself of the plague.

—Red Cultists are followers of VanDrac and attack with a vampiric dagger that heals them for half of the H-DMG they inflict (round up).

Section 6.0

Boarding the Ship

Thank goodness. The ship hasn't left yet. The Lost Waif looks like a rundown ramshackle ship. The paint is peeling if almost gone. The wood is splintered. The sails look tattered. You wonder if this ship could even make the trip across the ocean. In any case, you have to board.

You must now attempt a boarding action. As you rush out across the dock toward the ship you run into the Dock Master. "Where do you think you're going?" he demands. You must now make a CH roll to convince him to let you stow away. If you fail, you may spend 1 pound to reroll. You may do this as many times as you wish, so long as you still have money.

However, if you fail and don't have money (or choose not to bribe him) he turns you away.

Instead, you will need to make 2 successive DE checks. The first is to sneak past the Dock Workers. If you fail this roll, you must fight 1 Dock Worker (stats in the table from the previous section) and then try sneaking again once you've defeated the dock worker.

Once you pass, you will make a second DE check to swim to the ship and board. If you fail, you lose 1 will and try again. If you have no will, take 1 drowning damage and try again.

Once you pass, you finally board and hide away in a dark corner of the ship's Cargo Hold.

Section 7.0

Aboard the Lost Waif

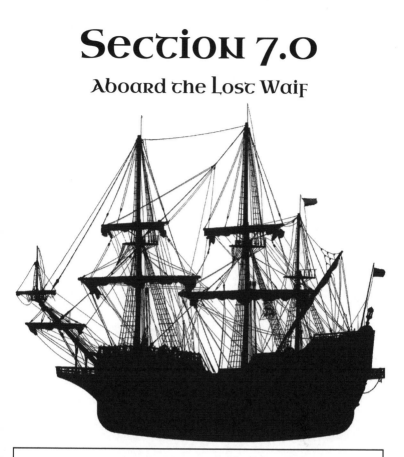

The stench of wet decay and rotted fish permeates the Cargo Hold. It takes all your strength to keep from throwing up. However, stifling the sickness, you manage to doze off. You wake up to the rocking of the waves and you realize the ship has disembarked. There doesn't seem to be a lot of movement above you, so you assume some of the crew has gone to bed. Now is your chance to search the boat for the bones of Lord VanDrac.

Lost Waif Special Rules:

The Lost Waif is a preconstructed dungeon map. It is broken up into 4 levels.

- The Cargo Hold (7.1)
- The Lower Decks (7.2)
- The Main Deck (7.3)
- The Quarter Deck (7.4)

Each room on a deck has a number. These numbers correspond with a specific entry in the section.

<u>Doors:</u> Whenever you move to a newly numbered room on the SAME deck, you will need to make a door roll.

<u>Moving Between Rooms:</u> Every single time you move from one room to another on a deck, you will need to make a DE check to move quietly without being seen or heard. This gets harder the higher you move up on the ship.

- The Cargo Hold +0 DE
- The Lower Decks +1 DE
- The Main Deck +2 DE
- The Quarter Deck +3 DE

If you pass, you move unseen. If you fail, roll on the monsters chart for the ship. Once combat ends, roll 1D6 to see if anyone else heard the commotion. On a roll of 1, you've been discovered! Roll on the monster chart again.

Moving Between Decks:

Each deck has stairs to the other decks. These are designated by arrows pointing up (to move up to the next deck) or down (to the deck just below). When you move between decks, make the same DE check, using the modifier for the deck above which you are moving to. Again, if you fail, roll on the monsters chart.

Searching for Bones

You start in Room #1 in the Cargo Hold. Whenever you are in a room, including room #1, and after reading the room's textbox (and fighting monsters if they appeared) you will make a WITS roll to search. If you fail, you will need to move on and come back later to try again. If you pass, mark the room with an S and roll 2D6 on adding the number of rooms marked with an S. If the score is 15 or more, you've found the coffin with the bones. Turn to section 8.0: Finding the Bones.

The Storm

As you travel over the sea, a large storm is kicking up. The storm can affect gameplay in several ways. The storm level begins at 1, but for each new room you enter you must roll 2D6 and consult the following tables to see if the storm level increases or decreases.

Storm Roll					
2-3	**4-5**	**6-7**	**8-9**	**10-11**	**12**
Storm Abates	Storm Steady	Storm Steady	Storm Worsens	Storm Worsens	Dark Tides
Storm -1	Storm +0	Storm +0	Storm +1	Storm +1	Storm +2

Each of the level effects stacks one on another as the storm level increases.

Storm Level		
1-3	Boat slightly rocky. No effect.	
4-6	Strong winds howl. +1 on bravery rolls.	
7-9	Loud thunder. Lose +1 Will in failed bravery.	
10-12	Ship rocks violently. +1 on all attack rolls.	
13-15	Cargo Hold flooded. Take 1D3 drowning damage when you enter a room.	When taking H-DMG on the Quarter Deck, make a DE check. If you fail, you go overboard.
16-19	Lower Deck flooded. Take 1D3 drowning damage when you enter a room.	When taking H-DMG on the Main Deck Area #2, make a DE check. If you fail, you go overboard.
20+	The Ship capsizes. You fail the mission.	

Ship Doorways		
6	**Open**	Move through freely.
4-5	**Stuck**	Must make a ST check to get through. Lose 1 WILL to reroll and try again.
1-3	**Locked**	Must make a DE check to dodge falling debris or take 1D6 H-DMG.

Ship Monsters

#	Monster	Max	H-DMG	W-DMG	LF
1	Sea Rat	6	1D2	1D3	2
2	Possessed Boatswain	4	1D3	1D2	5
3	Drowned Zombie	3	1D3	1D6	4
4	Vampiric Cabin Boy	2	1D6	1D6	10
5	Vampiric Crew	2	1D6+1	1D6	15
6	Vampiric Ship Captain*	1	2D6	1D6+2	20

Vampiric Powers

	Bloodletting	Power
Vampiric Cabin Boy	1	1
Vampiric Crew	1D2	1D2
Vampiric Ship Captain	1D3	1D3

The vampiric ship captain can only appear once. However, after he is killed all enemy damages increase by +1.

Section 7.1
The Cargo Hold

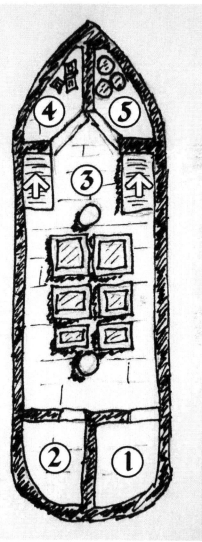

Room 1: Hold 1

You wake up to the rocking of the ship. It is dark and the hold you are in is damp and cold. You shiver, almost not wanting to get up, but you know you have to.

Make a ST check to ward off the cold. If you fail, take 1D3 H-DMG and 1D3 W-DMG. If you return to this room again, that strange chill returns and you will have to roll again.

Room 2: Hold 2

This hold is mostly empty but is almost identical to the one you stowed away in. Still, there isn't much here to search through.

The search check in this room is made at −1 to the WITS roll.

Room 3: Main Hold

This area is large and contains huge crates that almost reach the ceiling. You wonder what is in them. Make a WITS check. If you pass, read the text below this box. If you fail, skip it.

As you check the boxes, you see they are filled with earth. You know that vampires need to rest in their own native earth during the day. You begin to wonder how many vampires are on board this ship.

Room 4: Food Storage 1

This room contains crates of potatoes, onions, fish on ice, and other foods to feed the crew. Make a WITS check. If you pass, read the text below this box. If you fail, skip it.

On closer inspection, you realize the food is mostly rotting. Mold grows in fuzzy bunches on everything and some items are slimy. It seems the crew isn't concerned about eating. . . at least not normal food. The smell makes you want to throw up. Make a ST check or lose 1D2 health.

This room contains large barrels of liquid, probably wine for transport or for the crew to drink. Make a WITS check. If you pass, read the text below this box. If you fail, skip it.

On closer inspection, you realize the liquid isn't wine at all . . . but blood. Make a WITS check or lose 1D3 Willpower.

Section 7.2
The Lower Deck

Room 1: Cabin 1

This cabin on the back of the boat has one tiny window looking out at the ocean. As you peer out, you swear you can see a swarm of thousands of bats flying in the storm, almost as if they are making it.

Make a WITS check. If you fail take 1D6 W-DMG.

Room 2: Cabin 2

Instead of a bed, this cabin has a long box that resembles a coffin. If you open the box, read the text below.

The coffin appears empty. You let out a sigh of relief.

Room 3: Cabin 3

This cabin seems stuffed full of trinkets, baubles, and other items that seem to come from "the old world." Make a WITS to check to investigate them. If you fail, take 1D3 W-DMG. If you pass, read the text below.

Among the strange items is an old seeing crystal you might see a fortune teller use. Looking into the crystal, you see your future self. You are much stronger. Add +1 to your STR score.

Room 4: Cabin 4

Instead of a bed, this cabin has a long box that resembles a coffin. If you open the box, read the text below.

You open the coffin to reveal a young man inside. Make a DE check to stake him before he wakes up. If you fail, he jumps up and attacks you. Fight a Vampiric Cabin Boy.

Room 5: Cabin 5

This cabin contains an old cot and nothing more.

Nothing of consequence in his room.

Room 6: Cabin 6

This cabin has garlic strands hanging from the ceiling as well as crosses on every wall. However, the crosses have been turned upside down and the garlic is rotted. On the bed is a dead figure dressed like a captain. Make a WITS check. If you pass read the text below. If not, skip it.

You realize this must have once been the captain of this ship. He has been murdered. Whoever is acting captain is an imposter.

Room 7: The Galley

This room contains large long tables for the crewmen to eat at. However, it doesn't look like the tables have been used in a while. They are covered in dust. Make a WITS check. If you pass, read the text below. If not, skip it.

You manage to find a crust of bread on one of the tables that doesn't seem too stale or old.

Room 8: The Kitchen

This room is where food is prepared. Utensils, plates, and cups rattle in the cupboard. A large butcher's knife sits embedded in the huge cutting board.

If you take the knife, add it to your inventory. It does 1D3+2 damage in any given melee attack.

Section 7.3

The Main Deck

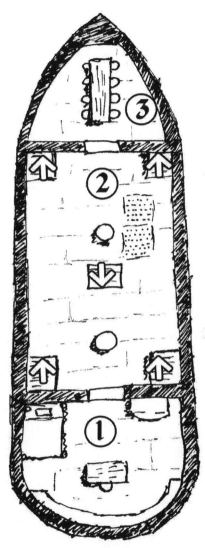

Room 1: Captain's Quarters

Compared to the rest of the ship, this room is decedent. It has a huge four-post bed with velvet red curtains on it. A desk of the finest wood sits at the center, topped with expensive trinkets and lavish maps of the ocean. A huge cabinet sits against the wall and it contains the finest clothing. A long bench lines the back of the ship, looking out through windows onto the ocean. However, as you explore, you hear a noise from behind the curtains of the bed.

If you have not encountered the Vampiric Captain yet, you encounter him now. He leaps out from behind the curtain.

Room 2: Main Deck

Rain pours down on you in torrents. You are immediately soaked through to the bone out here. You feel almost weak in the cold.

You take +1 H-DMG from all enemies here.

Room 3: Conference Room

This room contains a long table for meetings. Papers and maps are strewn about as if a meeting had just recently been held. Make a WITS check. If you pass, read the text below. If you fail, skip it.

Looking through the papers, you realize that there are detailed plans for Lord VanDrac's cult of followers, called the Cult of the Red Raven, outlined here. All the papers are stamped with the cult's official Raven symbol--which you gather is the original crest belonging to Lord VanDrac.

The plans involve transporting the Lord's Bones across the ocean. However, the plan involves the deliberate sinking of the ship. It will kill all the possessed and hypnotized crew members as well as destroy evidence of the cult's movements. They know your Order is onto them, and they are trying to shake you off their tail.

You refuse to let that happen. You are more determined than ever to find those bones.

Section 7.4

The Quarter Deck

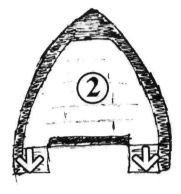

Room 1: The Stern

The rain and wind are gushing up here, making you feel off balance. You fear you may be blown right off into the ocean. As you move forward, you notice someone clinging to the ship's wheel. Make a WITS check, if you pass read the text below. If you fail, skip it.

Getting close, you realize that it is the dead body of the ship's original Second Mate. his limp limbs are tied to the wheel, keeping things steady.

Room 2: The Bow

You gasp at the cold and wet as you step up to the forward part of the ship. Looking out on the ocean you gasp. The front part of the ship is carved to look like a huge Raven, but it also looks like--in the darkness--a huge raven is guiding the ship through the night.

Make a WITS check. If you fail, take 1D6 W-DMG.

Section 8.0

Finding the Bones

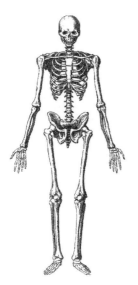

You stumble upon a small coffin, one you might assume was made for a child. Prying it open, you gasp. Inside is a cluttered mess of human bones ... including a skull with vampire fangs. You've found him. You've found Lord VanDrac. You wonder if it will be enough to just throw them overboard, but decide the best course would be to crush them to dust.

"I knew you'd find us, somehow," a familiar voice cries out over the storm. Turning, you see Father Tavers again.

"Surprised to see me?" the short hunchback chuckles, his eyes glowing red and his fangs glinting in the light. "I don't die easily."

"You're the leader of this Red Raven Cult," you assert.

"There are many leaders," he confesses, "I am but one. If I were to perish, someone else would step up." He drums his fingers along the long hilt of the ruby red scabbard of a sword. "But, enough is enough. I can no longer let you interfere. You can choose to join us as one of the damned . . . or perish by my hand." He draws the sword and points it at you.

"Not on your unlife," you whisper, charging into battle.

Monster	Max	H-DMG	W-DMG	LF
Father Tavers	1	2D6+1	2D6+1	30

Father Tavers Vampiric Power	Bloodletting	Power
	1D3+1	1D3+1

Once Father Tavers is defeated, read Section 9.0.

Section 9.0

Ending the Adventure

Gaining the upper hand, you rip the sword from the fat hunchback's grip. Before he can cry out his surprise, you make one final stroke. The blade meets flesh and cuts through, almost like butter, until his head disconnects from his shoulders. The head flies off into the night, blood trailing behind, and vanishes into the ocean. His body kneels, then topples over, blood pouring from the open neck wound and splashing your feet. "Let's see you come back from that," you spit.

However, before you can truly celebrate, you hear a deafening crack. The wood of the ship splinters around you. The whole thing is coming apart in the storm. You scramble to think of what to do next, but can't come up with any answers. No lifeboat will save you in this terrible storm. Soon, the boat is tilting and the ocean water is gushing toward you, filling the boat, covering the decks. Keeping a firm grip on the sword, you let the waves envelop you, embracing your fate.

You only pray that the bones of Lord VanDrac will be lost forever on the bottom of the ocean.

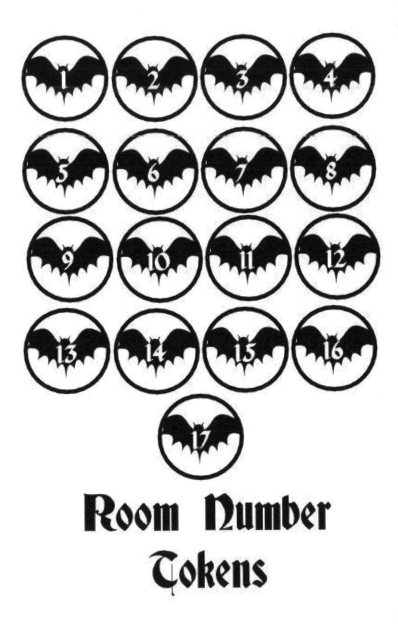

Room Number Tokens

Hammer✠Cross

Character Record Sheet

Name: **Order:**   **Class:**

STATS

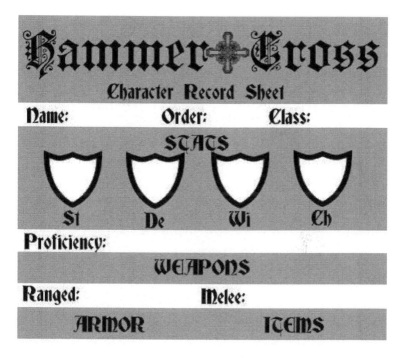

St   De   Wi   Ch

Proficiency:

WEAPONS

Ranged: **Melee:**

ARMOR   ITEMS

WILL   HEALTH   FAITH   £

Made in the USA
Monee, IL
12 August 2021